POETRY from Crescent Moon Publishing

Friedrich Hölderlin: *Hölderlin's Songs of Light: Selected Poems*
translated by Michael Hamburger

*German Romantic Poetry: Goethe, Novalis,
Heine, Hölderlin, Schlegel, Schiller*
by Carol Appleby

Cavafy: Anatomy of a Soul
by Matt Crispin

Rilke: Space, Essence and Angels in the Poetry of Rainer Maria Rilke
by B.D. Barnacle

Rimbaud: Arthur Rimbaud and the Magic of Poetry
by Jeremy Mark Robinson

Petrarch, Dante and the Troubadours: The Religion of Love and Poetry
by Cassidy Hughes

Dante: *Selections From the Vita Nuova*
translated by Thomas Okey

Arthur Rimbaud: *Selected Poems*
edited and translated by Andrew Jary

Arthur Rimbaud: *A Season in Hell*
edited and translated by Andrew Jary

Rainer Maria Rilke: *Dance the Orange:* Selected Poems
translated by Michael Hamburger

William Shakespeare: *Selected Sonnets and Verse*
edited, with an introduction by Mark Tuley

Edmund Spenser: *Poems*
selected and introduced by Teresa Page

Robert Herrick: *Selected Poems*
edited and introduced by M.K. Pace

Sir Thomas Wyatt: *Poems*
selected and introduced by Louise Cooper

John Donne: *Poems*
selected and introduced by A.H. Ninham

D.H. Lawrence: *Selected Poems*
edited with an introduction by Margaret Elvy

Percy Bysshe Shelley: *Poems*
selected and introduced by Charlotte Greene

Thomas Hardy: *Selected Poems*
edited, with an introduction by A.H. Ninham

Emily Bronte: *Poems*
selected and introduced by Teresa Page

John Keats: *Selected Poems*
edited with an introduction by Miriam Chalk

Henry Vaughan: *Poems*
selected and introduced by A.H. Ninham

The Crescent Moon Book of Love Poetry
edited by Louise Cooper

The Crescent Moon Book of Mystical Poetry in English
edited by Carol Appleby

The Crescent Moon Book of Nature Poetry From Langland to Lawrence
edited by Margaret Elvy

The Crescent Moon Book of Metaphysical Poetry
edited and introduced by Charlotte Greene

The Crescent Moon Book of Elizabethan Love Poetry
edited and introduced by Carol Appleby

The Crescent Moon Book of Romantic Poetry
edited and introduced by L.M. Poole

Blinded By Her Light The Love-Poetry of Robert Graves
by Jeremy Mark Robinson

The Best of Peter Redgrove's Poetry: The Book of Wonders
by Peter Redgrove, edited and introduced by Jeremy Mark Robinson

Peter Redgrove: Here Comes the Flood
by Jeremy Mark Robinson

Brigitte's Blue Heart
by Jeremy Reed

Claudia Schiffer's Red Shoes
by Jeremy Reed

By-Blows: Uncollected Poems
by D.J. Enright

*Shakespeare: Love, Poetry and Magic
in Shakespeare's Sonnets and Plays*
by B.D. Barnacle

ARSENY TARKOVSKY

LIFE, LIFE
SELECTED POEMS

ARSENY TARKOVSKY

LIFE, LIFE
SELECTED POEMS

TRANSLATED AND INTRODUCED BY
VIRGINIA ROUNDING

CRESCENT MOON PUBLISHING

CRESCENT MOON PUBLISHING
P.O. Box 393
MAIDSTONE
KENT
ME16 5XU, UK

First published 2000. Second edition 2007.
Introduction and translation © Virginia Rounding 2000, 2007.

Printed and bound in Great Britain.
Designed by Radiance Graphics, London.
Set in Monotype Goudy Modern.

The right of Virginia Rounding to be identified as translator of this book has been asserted generally in accordance with sections 77 and 78 of the Copyright, Designs and Patents Act 1988

All rights reserved. No part of
this book may be reprinted or reproduced, stored in a retrieval system, or transmitted, in any form or by any means, electronic, mechanical, photocopying, recording or otherwise, without permission from the publisher.

British Library Cataloguing in Publication data

Tarkovsky, Arseny
Life, Life: Selected Poems
1. Tarkovsky, Arseny – Translations into English
I. Title
891.7'144

ISBN 1-86171-114-X
ISBN 978-1-86171-114-4

CONTENTS

Author's Note
Introduction   17
Bibliography of Arseny Tarkovsky   23
Select Bibliography of Andrei Tarkovsky   25

Ignatyevo Forest   33
'I waited for you yesterday since morning'   34
Steppe   35
Joan's Tree   37
'May Vincent van Gogh forgive me'   39
The Way   40
Earthly   41
No. 10 of *Chistopol Notebook*   42
The Tailor From Lvov   43
'A blind man was travelling from Bryansk'   45
'I will dream on a black day'   46
The Sun's Eclipse, 1914   48
Objects   50
Butterfly   52
In Memory of Marina Tsvetayeva   53
First Meetings   59
Eurydice   61
Streetlamps   63
In Winter   64
Life, Life   65
Dreams   67
Two Japanese Tales   68
'In childhood I fell ill'   70
'Now the summer's over'   71
'And this I dreamt, and this I dream'   72

'My sight – my strength – grows dim'   73
'That man lived and died'   74
'The table is laid for six'   75
A Dedication   77
The Ring at the Door at Night   82
Psyche   83
'Death is a nobody, a clerk, a fool'   84

Illustrations   89

AUTHOR'S NOTE

Several of these translations have previously appeared in *Chapman, Connections, Modern Poetry in Translation, Poetry & Audience, The Rialto, Sphinx* and *Stone Soup*.

Arseny Tarkovsky and his son Andrei. Moscow, 1948.

INTRODUCTION

...poetry is everywhere, where the poet is life.

So writes Arseny Tarkovsky in his essay "What Goes Into My Understanding of Poetry", published in the second volume of his *Collected Works* (1991), and indeed the characteristic which comes across most strongly in his entire output, including in the poems chosen for this selection of translations, is this poet's love of life. As Kirill Kovaldzhi expresses it in his introduction to the *Collected Works*: 'He felt keenly the wonder of life and its element of tragedy, grasped its secret with the sober penetration of a scholar and the inspired vision of an artist.' This is no facile, sentimental love, but a commitment which demands everything from the lover. It is ex-pressed particularly strongly in the poem 'Earthly' (1960) where the poet rejects the idea of immortality and paradise in favour of 'earth's bile and salt'.

Arseny Aleksandrovich Tarkovsky was born in June 1907 in Elizavetgrad, later named Kirovograd. He studied at the Academy of Literature in Moscow from 1925 to 1929, and also worked in the editorial office of the journal *Gudok*. He was well respected as a translator, especially of the Oriental classics, but was little known as a poet for most of his life, being unable to get any of his own work published during the Stalinist era. His poems did not begin to appear in book form until he was over fifty. His son, the film director Andrei Tarkovsky, made extensive use of his father's poetry in some of his films, and certain of his diary entries indicate the esteem in which the poet was held in the Soviet Union towards the end of his life. An entry written after Andrei had given a talk at the Moscow Physical Institute in 1980, for instance, reproduces the following note from a member of the audience: 'An enormous number of people in this hall admire Arseny Aleksandrovich Tarkovsky as a great Russian poet. Please convey our respects to him.'[1] One of the few recorded public appearances of Arseny Tarkovsky was at the funeral of Anna Akhmatova; he was one of three writers deputed to accompany her coffin from Domodedovo to Leningrad, and he read both at her funeral in Komarovo and at the first evening held in her memory in Moscow. He died in 1989 and is now beginning to be recognised as one of the many significant Russian poets of the twentieth century.

In arranging the poems in this selection I have followed the order used in the first two volumes of the three-volume *Collected Works*. These include Tarkovsky's original verses and poems, his stories, re-collections, articles, and remarks about art and literature. The first volume contains poems from the collections published in the poet's lifetime, while the second brings together previously uncollected poems, some of which had appeared in various periodicals, others of which are published here for the first time, in addition to short stories and essays. The third volume includes selected translations by the poet.

One way in which Tarkovsky expresses his love of and commit-ment to life is by the attribution of human characteristics to nature. The sky shivers in 'Ignatyevo Forest' (1935); the earth has her own memory in 'Steppe' (1961) where the moon is asleep. In this latter poem Adam is pictured as having fulfilled more than his traditional role of naming animals and plants, 'bird and stone', for he has gone further and actually bequeathed consciousness to the natural world. And this, according to Tarkovsky, is the role of the poet. Kirill Kovaldzhi quotes him as saying: 'If you do not accept the role of the poet as a participant in the creation of life, then you cannot under-stand the essence of poetry.' Another poem concerning the role of the poet is 'Joan's Tree' (1959), which describes how the poet, like Joan of Arc, has learnt to hear voices, and not only to hear them, but to direct them as a conductor directs an orchestra. The voices come from nature and from the poet's experience of the world around him; his practice of listening to them, of transcribing them into poetry, means that his poetry does not belong to himself alone, was not invented by him, but is itself part of the world, beyond the individual. Moreover there is a suggestion that, like Joan, the poet will be sacrificed, but that he has to do what he does and that the outcome for him personally is really not the point. There is also a sense in some of nature, as depicted in, for instance, 'Butterfly' (1958), that it has come from elsewhere and knows something the poet does not know, so that his desire to put it into words, or give words to it, to 'put thought in this flesh', may be presumptuous.

The poem 'Objects' (1957) is another celebration, this time of – mainly – inanimate things which are yet part of what is to be loved about life. And another theme emerges which will be repeated – that of the continuance of life in future generations, and of the need for generosity in bequeathing the joys of life to one's children, grandchildren, even great-great-grandchildren, and not trying to cling on to them for oneself. This sense of bequeathing the future, life itself, to the next generations, attains its fullest expression in the poem 'A Dedication' (1934-1937).

There are towns for Tarkovsky which exist in the imagination, places of dream which he will recognise on arrival, and which seem to be awaiting him. In 'The Way' (1958) these 'sacred, unimagined towns' summon him; perhaps they represent his inspiration, or his calling, requiring him to use his poetic gift in an attempt to reach them. The poet writing a poem is like the railway engineer walking with his lamp through the darkness, keeping to the track down which the summons rings.

Marina Tsvetayeva is a striking presence in several of Tarkovsky's poems. The two poets became acquainted in 1939, soon after Tsvet-ayeva's return to the Soviet Union. Her first letter to him, written after he had sent her a book of his translations, concludes: 'Every manuscript is defenceless. I am all manuscript.' They soon became close friends, and Tarkovsky showed her several of his poems, sometimes taking her advice in making changes. He was about fifteen years younger than her; she seems to have fallen for him, imagining a grand passion. But Tarkovsky was already married, his wife resented Tsvetayeva, and he refrained from being all Tsvet-ayeva wanted him to be for her. Tarkovsky's poem which begins 'The table is laid for six' is associated with Tsvetayeva; her last fragment of poetry, discovered years after her death, was a response to this poem, accusing him of forgetting to lay a seventh place – for her. I would suggest that the poem 'Psyche' (April, 1941) is also associated with her, Tsvetayeva having often identified herself with this mythological character in her wanderings over the earth, her sense of homelessness after Eros has flown away and left her. On the afternoon of 31st August, 1941, Tsvetayeva was found hanging from a hook inside the entrance to her hut in Yelabuga, a small Tartar town in the Urals. The tenth poem (dated 28th November, 1941) of Tarkovsky's sequence entitled *Chistopol Notebook* recalls that place, and blames it for her death. She was buried there in an unmarked grave. The cycle which bears the dedication 'In memory of Marina Tsvetayeva (1939-1963)' celebrates her, both in life and death, insisting on the continuance of that memory.

Two of the poems in this selection touch on Tarkovsky's experience of war: 'The Tailor from Lvov' (1947) and 'A blind man was travelling from Bryansk' (1943). The poet was on active service during the Second World War; in 1943 he was severely wounded and had to have his right leg amputated. The threat, the darkness, of the times in which he lived are not absent from Tarkovsky's poetry, though neither are they an intrusive presence. Nothing deters his celebration of life. Perhaps the poem 'First Meetings' (1962) encapsulates his attitude. It is a wonderful ode to life, to love, nature, things and poetry, and yet it ends with a recognition of the tragedy of life, of the threat constantly posed by fate, the 'madman brandishing a razor', which cannot be escaped. 'In Winter' (1958) resonates with that same sense of threat, while 'The Ring at the Door at Night' (1946) reminds the reader of just how that threat was realised for so many people during the Stalinist era. But for Tarkovsky, ultimately, the joy of life is stronger than death: 'life is a wonder of wonders' and 'Death is a nobody'.

The poet's diction, like that of his greatest predecessor, Pushkin, is simple, though he does occasionally include archaisms. Certain words, certain images, occur again and again: ancestors, grandsons, beams of light, grasshoppers, wings, leaves, branches, candles, transparency, dust. All contribute to an overwhelming sense of this poet's love of life, his delight in the gift of sight, the bounties of the world spread out for him to choose from. As he himself put it in "What Goes Into My Understanding of Poetry": 'It is possible to learn to use rhythm, metaphor and so on, but that won't make you a poet, because poetry is a way of seeing, of selection and harmonisation. Only a seer can see, only one enriched by the world can select… There are no poets who have not loved life, however much they may have cursed her. She is their wet-nurse and their mother; moreover, she lavishly feeds their art with her plentiful bread and still lets them choose: this piece we will eat, and that piece we will scorn.'

NOTES

1. Andrei Tarkovsky, *Time Within Time: The Diaries, 1970-1986*, tr. Kitty Hunter-Blair, London, 1994, p. 229.

BIBLIOGRAPHY OF ARSENY TARKOVSKY

Lidiya Korneyeva Chukovskaya. *The Akhmatova Journals*, London, 1994
Kornei Chukovsky. *Lyudi i knigi*, Moscow, 1960
Elaine Feinstein. *A Captive Lion: Marina Tsvetaeva*, London, 1987
Max Hayward. *Twentieth-century Russian Poetry*, London, 1993
E.M. Olshankaya. "Anna Akhmatova i Arsenii Tarkovskii", in *Russian Literature*, xxx, 1991, pp. 373-84
Roberta Reeder. *Anna Akhmatova: Poet & Prophet*, London, 1995
Andrei Tarkovsky. *Time Within Time: The Diaries, 1970-1986*, tr. Kitty Hunter-Blair, London, 1994
Arseny Tarkovsky. *Blagoslovennyi svet*, St Petersburg, 1993
—. *Sobranie sochinenii* [*Collected Works*], 3 vols., Moscow, 1991-93
Victor Terras, ed. *Handbook to Russian Literature*, New Haven, CT, 1985

SELECT BIBLIOGRAPHY OF ANDREI TARKOVSKY

Compiled by Jeremy Mark Robinson

BY ANDREI TARKOVSKY

"Tarkovsky", *Kogda film okonchen* [*When the film is finished*], Iskusstvo kino, Moscow, 1964
interview, *Ekran*, 65, Sbornik, Iskusstvo, Moscow, 1966
"Zapechatlennoye vremya [Imprinted time]", *Iskusstvo kino*, 4, 1967
"Vsesoyuznaya pereklichka kinematografistov" ["An All-Union Filmmakers' Discussion]", *Iskusstvo kino*, 4, 1971
"Zachem proshloye vstrechayetsya s budushchim? [Why does the past meet the future?]", *Iskusstvo kino*, 11, 1971
Bely, bely den [*Bright, bright day*], Mosfilm, Moscow, 1973
"O Kinobraze [About the film image]", *Iskusstvo kino*, 3, 1979
"My delayem filmy [We make films]" *Kino*, Lithuania, 10, 1981
interview, *Time Out*, 568, Mch, 1981
interview, *Time Out*, 686, Nov, 1981
"Between Two Worlds", interview, *American Film*, Nov, 1983
interview, *Time Out*, 729, Aug, 1984
interview, *The Listener*, Aug, 1984
"A Propos du *Sacrifice*", *Positif*, 303, May, 1986
"Entretien", *Cahiers du Cinema*, 392, February, 1987
"Ya chasto dumayu o vas [I think of you often]", *Iskusstvo kino*, 6, 1987
Le Sacrifice, Schirmer, Munich, 1987
"Strasti po Andreyu [The passion according to Andrei]", interview, *Literaturnoye obozreniye*, 9, 1988
Zerkalo [*Mirror*], *Kinostsenarii*, 2, Goskino, 1988
"Krasota spasyot mir" ["Beauty will save the world"], *Iskusstvo kino*, 2, 1989
"Vstat na put [Taking the right path]", *Iskusstvo kino*, 2, 1989
Lektsii po kinorezhissure [Lecture on film directing[, ed. K. Lopushansky, Lenfilm, Leningrad, 1989
Martyrolog: Tagebücher, 1970-1986, tr. V. Schutz-Bischitzky & M. Milack-Verheyden, Limes, Berlin, 1989

Sculpting in Time: Reflections on the Cinema, tr. K. Hunter-Blair, Faber, London, 1989
Time Within Time: The Diaries, 1970-1986, tr. K. Hunter-Blair, Seagull Books, Calcutta, 1991
Andrei Rublev, tr. K. Hunter-Blair, Faber, London, 1991
Collected Screenplays, Faber, London, 1998
Der Spiegel. Filmnovelle, Arbeitstagebücher und Materialien zur Entstehung des Films, Limes Verlag, Berlin, 1993
Collected Screenplays, Faber, London, 1998
Andrei Tarkovski: Récits de jeunesse, Paris, 2004
Diaries, tr. C. Giroldi, ed. P. Rey, Cahiers du cinéma, Paris, 2004
Instant Light: Tarkovsky Polaroids, Thames & Hudson, , London, 2004
Interviews (Conversations with Filmmakers), 2006

ABOUT ANDREI TARKOVSKY

L. Alexander. "Never Be Neutral", *Sight & Sound*, January, 1997
C. Akesson. *The Sacrifice: The Film Companion*, I.B. Tauris, London, 2000
Andrej Tarkowskij, Reihe Film, 39, Carl Hanser Verlag, Munich, 1987
O. Assayas. "Tarkovsky: Seeing is Believing", *Sight & Sound*, January, 1997
H. Baba. *The Andrei Tarkovsky Films*, Misuzu Shobou, Tokyo, 2002
R. Bird. *Andrei Rublev*, British Film Institute, London
P. Christensen. "Kierkegaardian Motifs in Tarkovsky's *The Sacrifice*", *Soviet and East-European Drama, Theatre and Film*, 7, 2/3, Dec, 1987
I. Christie. "Raising the Shroud", *Monthly Film Bulletin*, February, 1987
—. "Returning to Zero", *Sight & Sound*, April, 1998
A. de Baecque. *Andrei Tarkovski*, Cahiers du Cinéma, Paris, 1989
M. Dempsey. "Lost Harmony: Tarkovsky's *The Mirror* and *The Stalker*", *Film Quarterly*, Autumn, 1981
N. Savio D'Sa. "Andrei Rublev: Religious Epiphany in Art", *Journal of Religion and Film*, 3, 2, 1999
T. Elmanovits. *The Mirror of Time: The Films of Andrei Tarkovsky*, Eesti Raamat, Tallinn, 1980
G. Gauthier. *Andrei Tarkovski*, Filmo, 19, Edilig, Paris, 1988
D.J. Goulding, ed. *Five Filmmakers: Tarkovsky, Forman, Polanski, Szabó, Makavejev*, Indiana University Press, Bloomington, IN, 1994
J. Graffy. "Tarkovsky: The Weight of the World", *Sight & Sound*, January, 1997
J. Grant. "Andrei Tarkovsky", *Cinéma*, 231, 1978
P. Green. "The Nostalgia of the Stalker", *Sight and Sound*, Winter, 1984-85
—. "Andrei Tarkovsky", *Sight and Sound*, 56, 2, Spring, 1987
—. *Andrei Tarkovsky*, Macmillan, London, 1993
S. Hancock. "Andrei Tarkovsky: Master of the Cinematic Image", *Mars Hill Review*, 1996

T. Hyman. "*Solaris*", *Film Quarterly*, Spring, 1976
E. Hynes. "Stalker", *Reverse Shot*, Spring, 2004
V.T. Johnson & G. Petrie. "Andrei Tarkovskii's Films", *Journal of European Studies*, 20, 3, September, 1990
—. *The Films of Andrei Tarkovsky. A Visual Fugue*, Indiana University Press, Bloomington, IN, 1995
G.A. Jonsson & T.A. Ottarsson. *Through the Mirror: Reflections on the Films of Andrei Tarkovsky*, 2006
W. Kaoru. *St. Tarkovsky*, Japan, 2003
H. Kennedy. "Tarkovsky: A Thought in Nine Parts", *Film Comment*, 23, 3, 46, 1987
B.A. Kovács & A. Szilágyi. *Les Mondes d'Andrei Tarkovski*, tr. V. Charaire, L'Age d'Homme, Lausanne, 1987
M. Le Fanu. *The Cinema of Andrei Tarkovsky*, British Film Institute, London, 1987
J. Leyda. *Kino: A History of the Russian and Soviet Cinema*, 3rd edition, Allen & Unwin, London, 1983
S. Martin. *Andrei Tarkovsky*, Essential Books, London, 2005
A. Mengs, *Stalker*, Ediciones Rialp, Spain
D. Miall. "The Self in History: Wordsworth, Tarkovsky and Auto-biography", *Wordsworth Circle*, 27, 1996
H. Marshall. "Andrei Tarkovsky's *The Mirror*", *Sight and Sound*, Spring, 1976
—. *Masters of the Soviet Cinema*, Routledge, London, 1983
M. McCormick. *Model of a House: An Essay on Andrei Tarkovsky's The Sacrifice*, 2006
V.I. Mikhalkovich. *Andrei Tarkovsky*, Znaniye, Moscow, 1989
T. Mitchell. "Tarkovsky in Italy", *Sight and Sound*, Winter, 1982-83
—. "Andrei Tarkovsky and *Nostalghia*", *Film Criticism*, 8, 3, 1984
I. Montagu. "Man and Experience: Tarkovsky's World", *Sight and Sound*, Spring, 1973
S. Nykvist. "Entretien" (with H. Niogret), *Positif*, 324, Feb, 1988
—. & B. Forslund. *In Reverence of Light*, Albert Bonniers Publishing Company, Sweden, 1997
A. Pavelin. *Fifty Religious Films*, A. P. Pavelin, Chiselhurst, Kent, 1990
S. Petraglia. *Andrej Tarkovskij*, Edizioni A.I.A.C.E., Turin, 1975
V. Petric. "Tarkovsky's Dream Imagery", *Film Quarterly*, Winter, 1990
L. Yan Pin. "Simvolika Tarkovskogom i daoizma [The symbolism of Tarkovsky and Taoism]", *Kinovedcheskiye zapiski*, 9, 1991
M. Ratschewa. "The Messianic Power of Pictures: The Films of Andrei Tarkovsky", *Cineaste*, 13, 1, 1983
J.M. Robinson. *The Sacred Cinema of A ndrei Tarkovsky*, Crescent Moon, 2006
J. Romney. "Future Soul [*Solaris*]", *Sight & Sound*, 2002
J. Rosenbaum. "Inner Space: Exploring Tarkovsky's *Solaris*", *Film Comment*, 26, 4, Aug, 1990
D. Salynsky. "Rezhissyor i mif [Director and myth]", *Iskusstvo kino*, 12, 1989
A.M. Sandler, ed. *Mir i filmy Andreya Tarkovskogo* [*The world and Films of Andrei Tarkovsky*], Iskusstvo, Moscow, 1991
V. Solovyov. "Semeynaya khronika ottsa i syna Tarkovskikh [The family chronicle of Tarkovsky's father and son]", *Novoye russkoye slovo*, May 12, 1989
P. Strick. "*The Sacrifice*", *Monthly Film Bulletin*, January, 1987

—. "Tarkovsky's Lost Minutes", *The Times*, July, 12, 989
—. "Releasing the Balloon, Raising the Bell", *Monthly Film Bulletin*, Feb, 1991
O. Surkova. "Avtobiograficheskiye motivy v tvorchestve Andreya Tarkovskogo [Autobiographic motifs in the creative work of Andrei Tarkovsky]", *Kinovedcheskiye zapiski*, Moscow, 9, 1991
—. *Tarkovsky and I*, Zebra E, Dekont, 2002
N. Synessios. *Mirror*, I.B. Tauris, London, 2001
M. Tarkovskaya, ed. *O Tarkovskom [About Tarkovsky]*, Progress Publishers, Moscow, 1989
M. Turoskaya. *Tarkovsky: Cinema as Poetry*, tr. N. Ward, ed. I. Christie, Faber, London, 1989
T. Vinokuroya. "Khozhdeniye po mukam *Andreya Rublyova* [The tormented path of *Andrei Rublyov*]", *Iskusstvo kino*, 10, 1989
J. Vronskaya. *Young Soviet Film Makers*, Allen & Unwin, London, 1972
F. Yermash. "On byl khudozhnik [He was an artist]", *Sovetskaya kultura*, 9 September, 1989 & 12 September, 1989
M. Zak. *Andrei Tarkovsky: Tvorchesky portret [Andrei Tarkovsky: an artistic portrait]*, Soyuzinformkino, Moscow, 1988
N. Zorkaya. "Zametki k portretu Andreya Tarkovskogo [Remarks towards a portrait of Andrei Tarkovsky]", *Kino panorama*, 2, 1977

POEMS

IGNATYEVO FOREST

The last leaves' embers in total immolation
Rise into the sky; this whole forest
Seethes with irritation, just as we did
That last year we lived together.

The path you take's reflected in our tear-filled eyes,
As bushes are reflected in the murky flood-lands.
Don't be difficult, don't touch, don't threaten,
Don't offend the forest silence by the Volga.

You can hear the old life breathing:
Clumps of mushrooms growing in damp grass –
Though gnawed to the very core by slugs,
They still inflame the skin.

All our past is like a threat –
Look, I'm coming, watch, I'll kill you!
The sky shivers and holds a maple, like a rose, –
May it burn still stronger – right into your eyes.

'I waited for you yesterday since morning'

I waited for you yesterday since morning,
They guessed you wouldn't come,
Do you remember the weather? Like a holiday!
I went out without a coat.

Today came, and they fixed for us
A somehow specially dismal day,
It was very late, and it was raining,
The drops cascading down the chilly branches.

No word of comfort, tears undried...

STEPPE

Earth swallows herself
And, knocking her head against the sky,
Patches the gaps in her memory
With humankind and grass.

Grass hides under the horse-shoes,
Soul in an ivory box;
Only word beneath the moon
Looms in the steppe

Which sleeps like a corpse.
Boulders on burial mounds –
Tsars playing at watchmen –
Drunk stupid on moonlight.

Word is the last to die.
When the drill of water pushes up
Through the subsoil's tough integument,
Sky will stir

And burdock's eyelash sigh,
Grasshopper's saddle flash,
Bird of the steppe comb,
Sleepy, its rainbow wing.

Then up to his shoulders in blue-grey milk
See Adam enter the steppe from paradise,
Restoring both to bird and stone

The gift of intelligent speech;

He recreated while they slept
Their palpitating names,
And now he breathes delirium of consciousness,
Loving, like soul, into grass.

JOAN'S TREE

They talk to me,
I don't hear what they say.
My soul is listening to itself, like Joan of Arc.
Such voices sing!

I've learnt to direct them,
So can summon flutes or harps,
Bassoons, at will. Sometimes I wake up
To find they've all been playing away for ages
And we've almost reached the end.

My greetings, tall trunk, elastic branches,
Your foliage of rust-specked green –
Mysterious tree from which the bird
Who sings the first note flies.

But I ought to seize a pencil,
Try to fix in words the kettledrum's low rumble,
The woodwind's hunting calls,
The showering springtime rush of bows, –
I understand what's happening:
My soul puts a finger to her lips –
Be still! Be silent!
                       And everything which makes death live
And complicates our life acquires a new,
Transparent, sudden meaning,
Obvious, like glass. And I am silent,
With none of me held back,

Absorbed in the funnel's mouth of morning noise.
This is why it turns out, when we die,
No word we wrote belonged to us,
That what before we thought of as ourselves
Is peacefully revolving,
Separate, beyond comparisons,
Not containing us.

Oh Joan, dear Joan, poor little Joan!
Suppose your king were crowned, –
So what? The magic oak tree sounds,
A voice says something,
But in a wrong-sized shirt
You're bright with fire.

'May Vincent van Gogh forgive me'

May Vincent van Gogh forgive me
For not being able to help him,

For never spreading leaves
For his feet on the burning path,

For not untying the laces
Of his dusty peasant boots,

For giving him no water in a heatwave,
For letting him shoot himself in hospital.

Standing here I lift my gaze
To see a cypress twisted like a flame.

Indigo and lemon yellow, –
These have made me what I am;

Otherwise I would have dropped my words,
Cast an alien burden from my shoulders.

This angelic coarseness by which
His paintstroke is related to my line

Leads his viewer and my reader
To where Van Gogh is breathing stars.

THE WAY

The black wind, like a robber,
Sings in a criminal tongue.
A railway engineer is walking
Through the steppe, with a lamp, alone.

Above the cleaving ribbon
The lamp swings in his hand,
Like the beating of wings in a dream
In the dead of night on a river.

In this cradling light, this yellow,
On the edge of the universe,
I recognise my native earth
By a solitary token.

A dim prophetic summons
Is ringing down the rails
From sacred, unimagined towns
Which never sleep at night.

And carefully, like an artist,
The traveller follows the light,
Until on the far horizon
The railwayman fades from sight.

EARTHLY

If I'd been destined at birth
    To lie in the lap of the gods,
I'd have been reared by a heavenly wet-nurse
    On the holy milk of the clouds.

I'd be god of a stream or a garden,
    Keeping watch over graves or the corn, –
But no – I'm a man, I don't need immortality:
    A heavenly fate would be awful.

I'm glad no one stitched my lips in a smile,
    Remote from earth's bile and salt.
So off you go, violin of Olympus,
    I can do without your song.

NO. 10 OF *CHISTOPOL NOTEBOOK*

I call – but Marina doesn't answer, she's asleep
In Yelabuga, Yelabuga of cemetery clay;

Your name should grace the good-for-nothing marsh,
Your bolt-like word should bar the gates;

Yelabuga – a threat to frighten unloved children,
Swindlers and robbers in your made-to-measure graves.

But whom instead did your ferocious coldness freeze?
For whom were you the final resting-place on earth?

Whose swan-like cry awakened you at dawn?
You heard the last word of Marina.

Now in your fatal wind I'm chilled as well.
Accursed place of fir trees, give me back Marina!

THE TAILOR FROM LVOV

(October, 1941)

Clutching a cardboard suitcase,
Leaning on a crooked stick,
Bowler-hatted, paddle-footed,
Beside himself, he paces the platform.

Possessed by a restless anguish,
He's without a ticket and has no answers.
Once upon a time he lived in a town —
Lodz perhaps, or was it Lvov?

He's trying to reach Kazan or Ufa —
'What torment this is, I swear it!
I'm all upside down, confused,
And not even dressed for a journey.'

Ears of an unreaped cornfield
Bend beneath scythes of fire.
For three whole days in this alien town
The past has been burning.

The carriages are crammed with people's commissars,
Hospital dressing-gowns,
The Japanese attaché —
No room for a living soul.

A sentry stands on guard,
The shelling has started again,
Fate like a black thread
Falls on the town.

Somehow he tapers the waistcoat,
Smelling of snow and fire,
While he drinks to overflowing
The wine of triumph in death.

An after-taste of decay
Lingers on his tongue,
It's as though he hears the king of kings
Calling to heaven from hell.

A beggar curls up in a goods van
Without a pillow or coat,
Without so much as a farthing —
The stranger, the refugee, the no one.

He stands above the frozen Kama.
Lvov is sleeping in its grave.
The son of grief is weeping,
The very lowest of her sons.

He would eat bread but there is no salt,
He would eat salt but there is no bread.
Soon snow will melt on the open field,
The track be overgrown with wormwood.

'A blind man was travelling from Bryansk in a goods van'

A blind man was travelling from Bryansk in a goods van,
Travelling home with his fate.

She was finding the words to console him —
'What are blindness and war after all?

It's lucky you're blind and a beggar,' she said,
'You'd never survive if you saw.

The Germans ignore you, you're nothing to them —
But own so much as that sack…

Carry that torn empty sack on your shoulders…
Just let me open your eyes…

A blind man was travelling home with his fate,
Content with that fate, and his blindness.

'I will dream on a black day'

I will dream on a black day
High stars,
A deep spring,
Cold water,
Crosses of lilac
In dew.
Nowhere to climb –
We are hidden in shade.

If ever a couple returned
To freedom from prison,
We did,
Alone in the world
And no longer children.
Am I not right
That your sleeve is more radiant
Than all?

Whatever befalls
On my blackest of days,
I will dream on that black day
A spring and the lilac,
A delicate ringlet,
Your simple attire;
On the bridge by the river
The wheels rattle by.

All ends in the world,
Even this night
Which carries you
Far from the garden.
Do we really have power
To bring back the dawn?
I gaze like a blind man
On happiness.

Someone is knocking. Who is it? Maria.
Open the door: who's there?
No reply. That's not
How the living arrive —
Their tread is heavier,
Their hands
Coarser and warmer
Than yours are, unseen.

Where have you been?
No answer.
Perhaps I dream
An indistinct rattle of wheels
On the bridge by the river
Where a star is shining,
A ringlet sinking forever,
A spring.

THE SUN'S ECLIPSE. 1914

That summer the national grief
Submitted to iron fetters,
By the edge of the very sea
The dusty steppe decayed.

At dusk the bitter distances –
A shifting summer soul –
Pulsated red-faced with anxiety,
Hurling abuse at God.

But by morning a deserter
Came barefoot to the village,
A dark and hungry face,
An off-white soldier's blouse.

He looked like a holy icon
As he gazed at the diamond sickle
Glittering into decline
On the rusty hem of the sky.

I learnt that motionless stare by heart,
Its origin some other kingdom;
In eyes scorched by war
I acknowledged the stranger.

The darkness expanded.
In a sleep-like green silence
He left and on leaving

Gave me his rifle.

If only I had recognised
The blinding light at once…

———————

How much I've lived through on earth!
Whole centuries! Millennia!

OBJECTS

Objects which shared my childhood
Keep on disappearing:
Lightning lamps and black gunpowder,
Dark water from the well,

Plush red divans and decadent-
Framed Islands of the dead,
Men with moustaches, old photographs,
Aeroplanes made out of reeds,

Nadson's consumptive three-parters,
Adonis-like lawyers in morning-coats,
The peculiar smell of galoshes,
Shoulders sloping from ostrich-like necks,

The curlicues of drunken symbolists,
Platitudes of strapping futurists,
Slogans on lime and chestnut trees,
Gangsters' imbecilic shotguns,

The hard sign and the letter yat —
One disappeared, the other altered —
And where there never used to be a comma
Now death intervenes as well.

I've done so little for the future,
Though the future's all I crave.
I don't want to start all over again

As if I've been wasting my time.

But there's no guarantee
I can play with the modern inventions —
I'm stepping on my grandson's baubles,
My great-great-grandson's glory.

BUTTERFLY

The butterfly flits
Through gradations of light,
A fleeting vision
On fire.

A book of wonders
Spread in the meadow,
Sky-powder wings
Painted blue.

Pure little bubble
Of butterfly-chrysalis,
Otherworld blood
In its belly –

I'd put thought
In this flesh… dare I
Finger the sinews
Of Pharaoh?

IN MEMORY OF MARINA TSVETAYEVA

I FROM AN OLD NOTEBOOK

Everything real communicated — the air
Around you to the very stars,
Your small waist, each of your elastic
Stubborn steps, your cornered verse.

You aren't on bail,
Free to blaze and squander,
Don't acknowledge any parting,
The times close up like water.

Assent to joy and sadness!
Leave the furled wings undisturbed:
Supreme above the waters of disaster,
Don't wrench the waves apart.

II WASH-DAY

Marina is doing the laundry.
Aloof, her worker's hands
Fling sparkling suds
At the naked wall.

She wrings out the linen.
Hangs up her dress
In the wide-open window.
Witness the crucified.

An aeroplane drones overhead,
Foam subsides in the basin,
The afternoon's ripped into rags
By the wail of an air-raid siren.

Grey dress in the window.
Distance grows dark to the door.
Marina is dappled with green –
As though submerged in a river.

Two months to go. She flings back
The hair from her forehead.
Thereafter the mistress is fate,
Most stubborn of women...

III

Friends, lovers of truth,
Of times extinguished by death,
What did Tsvetayeva read to you,
Walking back from her funeral?

Hair dusted with clay,
And hand more yellow,
The far away voice
Too quiet to hear.

Is her edict to reach up
On tiptoe, seizing the stress?
To hurtle at uneven lines,
Not pausing for breath?

What was it she thought of?
What last words by the river
At that bitter, still summery
Burning time of the earth,

Like a widow leading soldiers
To the war, like a mother,
When it never was the custom
To comfort strangers?

In all your power, with all the field,
You stand behind the final line –
Mistaken in your righteousness,
Upright in your error.

IV

I'm listening, I'm not sleeping, you call me, Marina,
You warn with your wing, you sing to me, Marina,
While angels play their serenades above the town,
Irrevocably bitter
You bear our poisoned bread to Judgment Day,
As exiles took their fathers' ashes from Jerusalem,
When David wrote the psalms,
The enemy pitched his tent on Mount Sion.
Your dying summons echoes in my ear —
On the wild horizon past the darkened cloud
Your wing is flaming with prophetic fire.

V TWENTY-TWO YEARS?

All who live are dying, every
Blade of grass is trodden down and burnt,
Yet even in the midst of all this wailing
One death shrieks more clear than any other.

Why wasn't I, an arrow, consumed by fire?
Why haven't I completed my trajectory?
Why does life, a swift, still tremble
In my palms? Where is my dearest friend,

My godhead, angel of truth and anger?
To the right and the left there is blood,
But your bloodless death is a hundred times worse.
War shot me forth from his bowstring,
And I won't close your eyes.
But what did I do to be guilty?

VI TWENTY-TWO YEARS

Not speech — no, I don't want
Your treasures — vows and laments —
I won't re-educate the pen
Or modify the throat;

Not courage in the face of death —
In your notebooks you embodied
All ideas to the margin
Where your ink ran out;

Not primogeniture — I give away
My own, so on a surplus day
They'll give to you, in earth,
Your right of earthly glory;

Not the daring of your passions,
Nor the fact that all is one —
Teach, Marina, from the grave
Only of your memory.

I'm so afraid of forgetting you —
Of exchanging in a moment
The shining filament of your body
For the doubling and tripling
Of rhymes — so burying you
A second time inside your poetry.

FIRST MEETINGS

We celebrated every moment
Of our meetings as epiphanies,
Just we two in all the world.
Bolder, lighter than a bird's wing,
You hurtled like vertigo
Down the stairs, leading
Through moist lilac to your realm
Beyond the mirror.

When night fell, grace was given me,
The sanctuary gates were opened,
Shining in the darkness
Nakedness bowed slowly;
Waking up, I said:
'God bless you!', knowing it
To be daring: you slept,
The lilac leaned towards you from the table
To touch your eyelids with its universal blue,
Those eyelids brushed with blue
Were peaceful, and your hand was warm.

And in the crystal I saw pulsing rivers,
Smoke-wreathed hills, and glimmering seas;
Holding in your palm that crystal sphere,
You slumbered on the throne,
And — God be praised! — you belonged to me.
Awaking, you transformed
The humdrum dictionary of humans

Till speech was full and running over
With resounding strength, and the word *you*
Revealed its new meaning: it meant *king*.
Everything in the world was different,
Even the simplest things — the jug, the basin —
When stratified and solid water
Stood between us, like a guard.

We were led to who knows where.
Before us opened up, in mirage,
Towns constructed out of wonder,
Mint leaves spread themselves beneath our feet,
Birds came on the journey with us,
Fish leapt in greeting from the river,
And the sky unfurled above...

While behind us all the time went fate,
A madman brandishing a razor.

EURYDICE

A person has one
Body, like a solitary.
The soul is repelled
By the unbroken casing
With its ears, and eyes
The size of a coin
And, dressing the skeleton,
Scar upon scar of the skin.

The soul flies through the eye
Into the heavenly brook,
On to an icy cogwheel
Of a bird's chariot
And it hears through the bars
Of its living prison
The rattle of forests and corn-fields,
The trump of the seven seas.

The soul is sinful without the body,
Like the body without a night-shirt, —
No thought or deed,
Design or line.
Here's a riddle without a solution:
Who will return
Having danced on the platform
Where nobody dances?

And I dream of another
Soul, differently clothed:
It burns, as it passes
From shyness to hope,
It encircles the earth,
In liquid fire, without shadow,
Like the cluster of lilac
Left on the table.

Run, my child, don't lament
Over poor Eurydice;
Drive your copper hoop
With a stick round the world,
While in answer to each step —
Even though you don't hear it —
Both happy and dry
The earth sounds in your ears.

STREETLAMPS

I can't forget the thaw
This early bitter spring:
The drunken wind at a run
Lashed icy sleet in my face,
Nature, stripped of white garments,
Rubbed uncomfortably close,
And shaggy waters whinnied
Beneath the bridges' iron gloom.

What did you signify, what portend,
Streetlamps under the rain?
What griefs have you brought
On the town in your madness?
Why is the citizen anxious?
What insult has hurt him?
Why does your shining distress him?

Perhaps he's filled with longing like me:
We stare at the lead-coloured wave
As it sucks at the base of the pier
And we're hypnotised, numbed by your flicker,
The duplicitous dreams you command —
So come summer, in docile agreement
We'll relinquish the ebony spring.

IN WINTER

Where is fate – my girlfriend –
Leading? We shuffle along,
Losing the circle's edge
And stumbling over coffins.

We can't see the moon overhead,
Our crutches get stuck in the snow,
And white-eyed souls are peering at us
Along the ground.

Tell me, old woman, do you remember,
How you and I went walking
One frozen winter, at dead of night,
Beneath this same stone wall?
It was long long ago, but just as deeply,
Half aloud, a quarter audible,
The echo boomed behind our backs.

LIFE, LIFE

1   I don't believe in omens or fear
Forebodings. I flee from neither slander
Nor from poison. Death does not exist.
Everyone's immortal. Everything is too.
No point in fearing death at seventeen,
Or seventy. There's only here and now, and light;
Neither death, nor darkness, exists.
We're all already on the seashore;
I'm one of those who'll be hauling in the nets
When a shoal of immortality swims by.

2   If you live in a house – the house will not fall.
I'll summon any of the centuries,
Then enter one and build a house in it.
That's why your children and your wives
Sit with me at one table, –
The same for ancestor and grandson:
The future is being accomplished now,
If I raise my hand a little,
All five beams of light will stay with you.
Each day I used my collar bones
For shoring up the past, as though with timber,
I measured time with geodetic chains
And marched across it, as though it were the Urals.

3   I tailored the age to fit me.
    We walked to the south, raising dust above the steppe;
    The tall weeds fumed; the grasshopper danced,
    Touching its antenna to the horse-shoes — and it
                                         prophesied,
    Threatening me with destruction, like a monk.
    I strapped my fate to the saddle;
    And even now, in these coming times,
    I stand up in the stirrups like a child.

    I'm satisfied with deathlessness,
    For my blood to flow from age to age.
    Yet for a corner whose warmth I could rely on
    I'd willingly have given all my life,
    Whenever her flying needle
    Tugged me, like a thread, around the globe.

DREAMS

Night settles down by the window,
Puts on her magical glasses,
Intones the Babylonian dream-book,
In a singsong voice, like a priest.

Her footsteps lead away upward,
No rails on the stairwell of nothingness,
Where shades stand in ritual judgment.
Your mind belongs elsewhere.

Nothing makes sense or adds up.
Who are these judges? And how have you sinned?
Don't we all come from the cave?
Cuneiform differs for no one.

We are doomed to witness reality
From Euclid back to the Flood.
Return what you took; reveal what you saw!
Your offspring demand it.

You'll find shelter at last
On some threshold or other,
While bulls stroll along like gods,
Chewing the cud of time.

TWO JAPANESE TALES

I   THE POOR FISHERMAN

    I used to be a fisherman,
    But my nets were carried
    Out to sea. Now on earth
    I'm empty and transparent.

    My delight
    Rests in my poverty.
    From people
    I need nothing.

    Through the universe
    I'll journey, humble,
    Silent and barefoot,
    Following the sacred
    Star of the morning.

II THE FLUTE

I heard
A dying call,
An orphan flute
Beyond forests.

The willow bows
To the stream,
And the stream is babbling
Of nothing.

Note-perfect,
It spins to the top,
Then sinks to the bed.

'In childhood I fell ill'

In childhood I fell ill
From fear and hunger. Peeling
The crust from my lips, I licked them;
Memorised the fresh and rather salty taste.
And always I am walking, walking, walking,
I sit on the front stairs, trying to get warm,
I walk myself into delirium, like following
The Pied Piper into the river, I sit down on the stairs
Trying to get warm; I feel so shivery.
And my mother stands there, beckoning, she seems
Quite close, but I can't reach her:
I'm almost there — she stands seven steps away
And beckons; I'm almost there — she stands
Seven steps away and beckons. I've grown
So hot, I unbutton my collar and lie down, —
Now trumpets start to blare, light strikes
My eyelids, horses gallop by, my mother
Flies above the road, and beckons —
And then she flew away…
                        And now beneath the apple trees
I dream of a white hospital,
A white sheet covering my throat,
A doctor in a white coat looks at me
And at the foot a sister all in white
Is fluttering her wings. They stayed.
My mother came, and beckoned —
She flew away…

'Now the summer's over'

Now the summer's over,
As though it was never.
It's warm in the garner.
But that's not enough.

All I could wish for,
Like a four-leafed clover,
Fell into my hands,
But it's never enough.

Neither good nor evil
Happened in vain,
All shone brightly,
But it isn't enough.

Life took me under her wing,
Protected and saved me,
I've had all the luck.
But it's never enough.

The leaves were unscorched,
The branches unbroken…
The day is washed clean like a glass —
But that's not enough.

'And this I dreamt, and this I dream'

And this I dreamt, and this I dream,
And some time this I will dream again,
And all will be repeated, all be re-embodied,
You will dream everything I have seen in dream.

To one side from ourselves, to one side from the world
Wave follows wave to break on the shore,
On each wave is a star, a person, a bird,
Dreams, reality, death — on wave after wave.

No need for a date: I was, I am, and I will be,
Life is a wonder of wonders, and to wonder
I dedicate myself, on my knees, like an orphan,
Alone — among mirrors — fenced in by reflections:
Cities and seas, iridescent, intensified.
A mother in tears takes a child on her lap.

'My sight – my strength – grows dim'

My sight – my strength – grows dim,
Two invisible diamond lances;
My hearing fades to distant thunder
And the breathing of my father's house;
The knots of rigid muscles slacken,
Like grey oxen in a ploughed up field;
And the two wings at my shoulders
No longer shine at night.

I'm a candle burnt out at the feast.
Collect my wax in the morning
And you'll find this page will tell you
How you might cry and what to be proud of,
How to give away the final third
Of happiness, how to die easy,
And beneath a fortuitous roof
To blaze after death, like the word.

'That man lived and died'

That man lived and died,
So lived and died that woman,
These other people too:
All packed together in one grave.

Earth has more transparency than glass,
You can witness who was killed,
Who did the killing: on lifeless dust
The mark of good and evil glows.

Above the earth the shades of generations
Buried in the earth are troubled;
They'd find no hiding place
If we had leave to lynch them,
But where could such a court be found?
God knows we don't expect one.

'The table is laid for six'

> *Your native Slavyansk*
> *Is chalk and salt,*
> *I'm weary of solitude –*
> *Come sit with me...*

The table is laid for six,
With crystal and roses,
But my guests include
Sorrow and grief.

My father's here too,
And so is my brother.
An hour goes by.
A knock at the door.

Like twelve years ago,
A cold hand in greeting,
The rustle of blue
Unfashionable silks.

A tinkling of wine,
A ringing of glass:
'How we once loved you,
How the years fled!'

My father will smile,
My brother pour wine,

She'll give me her hand —
No rings — and she'll say:

— My shoes are worn out,
My plait has gone grey,
Our voices are singing
From under the earth.

A DEDICATION

I

The crowns of trees inhabit me —
Their confused distress, awake at night —
Like poetry I foretell the features
Pertaining to people and things.

Because I breathed as breathes the word,
Among the schoolboys I was echo —
A voice that chimed forsaken,
Alien in a voices' chorus.

Like a seven-year-old boy, the world can change,
Sleep like a baby when the storm's in bloom;
But a burden of inherited mistakes
In those days pressed on my palms.

My whole life turned up and stood in line
As though many years had gone by,
And the mirror gave answer
With a strange greenish glare.

I shuddered at every false sound,
I thought: I must empty my hands.
And on waking I set myself free
For learning to speak once again.

Nervous, I groped round for subjects —
Medusas in glimmering waters,
Roots of a tree warmed by music,
Marble flung back at a star.

I learnt to speak as in childhood,
Tongue-tied, tormented by stammers.
If the children would only recall their inheritance,
I'd leave them all that I have.

II

And each will remember the radiant town of childhood,
The hamlet in the mountains, the village by the river,
Where we took from our fathers as our birthright
The love of earth, forever dear.

Where mothers watched our cradles through the night,
Where we pored over books,
Our young minds seething
With inspiration's dawn.

Where we knew first love, not daring to declare it,
Where we grew up fighting,
Where we vowed before our conscience
Inviolable fidelity to you...

The trees in the avenue rustle
Like green torches of fire.
I give them away, you need them more —
Come, take the trees which I offer.

Take my whole town, it's all yours —
You'll fall asleep in my grass.
My swallows will warble to wake you —
I give them away, you need them more.

Prolonging the wonder, keeping the shades' agreement,
You'll summon all that I've lived by
For so many years far from here,
So many miles from your memory.

I'm the first guest on your birthday,
Granted the gift of living with you,
Of stepping into your dreams at night,
Of being reflected in your mirror.

III

It stretches out like a cobweb —
The remnant of all I used to love —
And I'm terrified of leaving to my heirs
Only an imaginary imprint.

Maybe children playing
Will remember me in passing
And confuse my incoherent interjections
With words denoting blindness.

I wasn't blind. I saw it all —
What had happened to the life of my contemporaries,
How its signature was verified by time

For slipping past blind sleepy eyes.

I saw everything there was to see,
Like the light of dawn through interlacing branches.
So take the bitterness too; in vain we try
To hide it from our sons and daughters.

IV

So I learnt to speak all over again,
Accepting the arduous gift in a menacing year,
When love scorched my cheeks,
Death's frost squeezed my heart.

Jealousy stood at my bedside,
Whispering in my ear:
                              — Look,
While you sleep, entangled in love,
The streetlamps have all gone out.

Trust me, I'll open your eyes:
Then you'll always be free;
In the rosy dawn your ultimate star
Is spreadeagled on the pavement...

So I ran from my threshold —
The light cuffed me awake,
Fear chased me all round the town —
I saw the lightning interlace.

Over the deserted square, into the distance,
The flashes flew like a flock of swans —

At least a hundred, I didn't count —
The height fluttering in their bills.

They flew so slowly I couldn't help feeling —
Despite the new day shining slap in my face —
That this bitterness might last forever,
Their reflections keeping us company.

So take them, you need them more —
Stroke them with a child's hand tenderly,
And especially the jealousies —
Then love will come easy.

V

And the sky, turning blue, came to life,
The height beginning to sink,
The wooden blocks of an arching bridge
Yielded to the first tram's wheels.

And while your gigantic town
Is rising green in the dawn, —
You lie, my child, in your mother's womb
In a bubble, soft, half-transparent.

And perhaps you see nothing,
But the sun drifts above you…

THE RING AT THE DOOR AT NIGHT

Why have you put up your chain
For the night, like a prisoner,
Ivan Ivanych? I'm standing outside
Your door while you sleep.

Killer-night, in black rubber shoes,
Is on its way to get me.
I'm ringing your bell to beg for shelter —
I can tell you don't want to help.

You've blocked up your ears with cotton wool
And hear the muffled ringing through your sleep.
Damn him, you say, let him scrabble about,
You think it's a sign of the times!

You don't believe in hell or look for paradise —
And if they don't exist, then what's the point?
Whatever will you say if I stain
Your threshold with my blood?

How can you leave for work at half-past eight
To earn your healthy salary
When you've betrayed your brother and your friend?
How can you just go walking down the street?

That street is turning black with blood,
The cross is daubed on every house.
'What are you going on about?' I hear you say,
'I didn't get this sleep for free — I've earnt it.'

PSYCHE

I can't forget the image of Cupid and the tender Psyche... (Afanasy Fet, 1820-92)

A beggar with a sweet tooth — that's who I am,
Dazzled by a kopek far more than by the sun —
So don't begrudge me a nut from the forest,
Spare a few sunflower seeds for the old.

Give homeless little Psyche something to munch on!
Open up, mother earth, grant me protection, —
Little boys keep setting the dogs on me,
I've no residence permit for this world.

I'd climb into the mountains but the slopes are too steep,
I'd denounce someone but I can't identify the culprit,
Like a fool I'd untwine my grey plaits,
But I've forgotten the name of my lover.

I'd wash the wings of my dear with tears,
By the paths of the swan I'd fly after him,
Above forests he'd feed me with honey,
Above mountains we'd sip heaven's wine.

He unfurled his bright wings — I remembered... too late:
The ferocious blizzard blew our love-nest away.
So I wander the world like a cast-off farm woman —
A lost soul, without papers, unclothed, with no shoes...

'Death is a nobody, a clerk, a fool'

Death is a nobody, a clerk, a fool,
A skinflint, a drooping hem,
Her mansion is a register office,
The clerk's stool is her throne.

The word freezes on the client's lips,
His mouth wide open, fish-like;
If death, alias our Mrs Jones,
Turns the calculator's handle,

She'll take the numbered file and burn
All the bitter torment of the soul
And, wielding a blue pencil,
Obliterate the idiotic flourish.

ILLUSTRATIONS

Two pages each from Andrei Tarkovsky's seven feature films: *Ivan's Childhood. Andrei Roublyov, Solaris, Mirror, Stalker, Nostalghia* and *The Sacrifice*

J.R.R. Tolkien
The Books, The Films, The Whole Cultural Phenomenon

by Jeremy Mark Robinson

A new critical study of J.R.R. Tolkien, creator of Middle-earth and author of *The Lord of the Rings*, *The Hobbit* and *The Silmarillion*, among other books.

This new critical study explores Tolkien's major writings (*The Lord of the Rings*, *The Hobbit*, *Beowulf: The Monster and the Critics*, *The Letters*, *The Silmarillion* and *The History of Middle-earth* volumes); Tolkien and fairy tales; the mythological, political and religious aspects of Tolkien's Middle-earth; the critics' response to Tolkien's fiction over the decades; the Tolkien industry (merchandizing, toys, role-playing games, posters, Tolkien societies, conferences and the like); Tolkien in visual and fantasy art; the cultural aspects of The Lord of the Rings (from the 1950s to the present); Tolkien's fiction's relationship with other fantasy fiction, such as C.S. Lewis and *Harry Potter*; and the TV, radio and film versions of Tolkien's books, including the 2001-03 Hollywood interpretations of *The Lord of the Rings*.

This new book draws on contemporary cultural theory and analysis and offers a sympathetic and illuminating (and sceptical) account of the Tolkien phenomenon. This book is designed to appeal to the general reader (and viewer) of Tolkien: it is written in a clear, jargon-free and easily-accessible style.

754pp   ISBN 1-86171-057-7   £25.00 / $37.50

The Best of Peter Redgrove's Poetry
The Book of Wonders

by Peter Redgrove, edited and introduced by Jeremy Robinson

Poems of wet shirts and 'wonder-awakening dresses'; honey, wasps and bees; orchards and apples; rivers, seas and tides; storms, rain, weather and clouds; waterworks; labyrinths; amazing perfumes; the Cornish landscape (Penzance, Perranporth, Falmouth, Boscastle, the Lizard and Scilly Isles); the sixth sense and 'extra-sensuous perception'; witchcraft; alchemical vessels and laboratories; yoga; menstruation; mines, minerals and stones; sand dunes; mud-baths; mythology; dreaming; vulvas; and lots of sex magic. This book gathers together poetry (and prose) from every stage of Redgrove's career, and every book. It includes pieces that have only appeared in small presses and magazines, and in uncollected form.

'Peter Redgrove is really an extraordinary poet' (George Szirtes, *Quarto* magazine)
'Peter Redgrove is one of the few significant poets now writing... His 'means' are indeed brilliant and delightful. Technically he is a poet essentially of brilliant and unexpected images...he never disappoints' (Kathleen Raine, *Temenos* magazine).

240pp   ISBN 1-86171-063-1   2nd edition   £19.99 / $29.50

Sex–Magic–Poetry–Cornwall
A Flood of Poems

by Peter Redgrove. Edited with an essay by Jeremy Robinson

A marvellous collection of poems by one of Britain's best but underrated poets, Peter Redgrove. This book brings together some of Redgrove's wildest and most passionate works, creating a 'flood' of poetry. Philip Hobsbaum called Redgrove 'the great poet of our time', while Angela Carter said: 'Redgrove's language can light up a page.' Redgrove ranks alongside Ted Hughes and Sylvia Plath. He is in every way a 'major poet'. Robinson's essay analyzes all of Redgrove's poetic work, including his use of sex magic, natural science, menstruation, psychology, myth, alchemy and feminism.
A new edition, including a new introduction, new preface and new bibliography.

'Robinson's enthusiasm is winning, and his perceptive readings are supported by a very useful bibliography' (*Acumen* magazine)
'*Sex-Magic-Poetry-Cornwall* is a very rich essay... It is like a brightly-lighted box. (Peter Redgrove)
'This is an excellent selection of poetry and an extensive essay on the themes and theories of this unusual poet by Jeremy Robinson' (*Chapman* magazine)

220pp   New, 3rd edition   ISBN 1-86171-070-4   £14.99 / $23.50

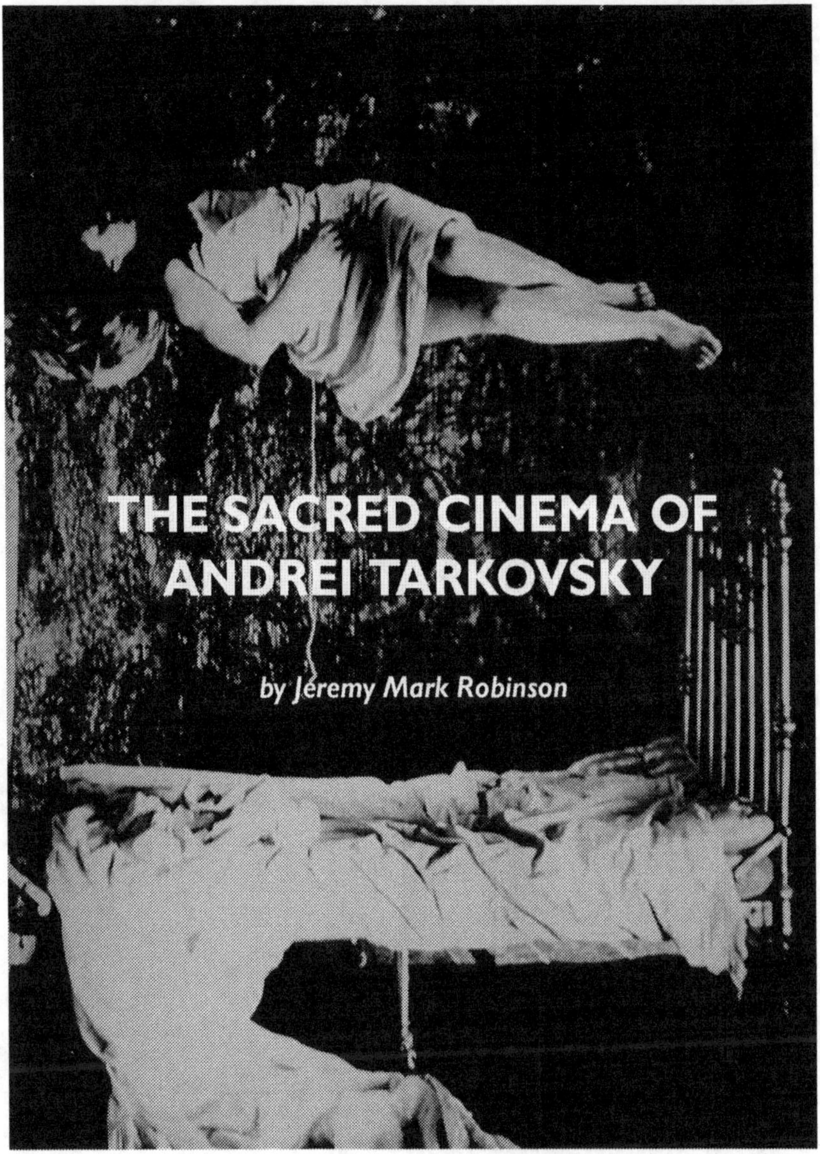

THE SACRED CINEMA OF ANDREI TARKOVSKY

by Jeremy Mark Robinson

A new study of the Russian filmmaker Andrei Tarkovsky (1932-1986), director of seven feature films, including *Andrei Roublyov, Mirror, Solaris, Stalker* and *The Sacrifice*.

This is one of the most comprehensive and detailed studies of Tarkovsky's cinema available. Every film is explored in depth, with scene-by-scene analyses. All aspects of Tarkovsky's output are critiqued, including editing, camera, staging, script, budget, collaborations, production, sound, music, performance and spirituality. Tarkovsky is placed with a European New Wave tradition of filmmaking, alongside directors like Ingmar Bergman, Carl Theodor Dreyer, Pier Paolo Pasolini and Robert Bresson.

An essential addition to film studies.

Illustrations: 150 b/w, 4 colour. 682 pages. First edition. Hardback.

Publisher: Crescent Moon Publishing. Distributor: Gardners Books.

ISBN 1-86171-096-8 (9781861710963) £60.00 / $105.00

THE ART OF ANDY GOLDSWORTHY

COMPLETE WORKS: SPECIAL EDITION
(PAPERBACK and HARDBACK)

by William Malpas

A new, special edition of the study of the contemporary British sculptor, Andy Goldsworthy, including a new introduction, new bibliography and many new illustrations.

This is the most comprehensive, up-to-date, well-researched and in-depth account of Goldsworthy's art available anywhere.

Andy Goldsworthy makes land art. His sculpture is a sensitive, intuitive response to nature, light, time, growth, the seasons and the earth. Goldsworthy's environmental art is becoming ever more popular: 1993's art book *Stone* was a bestseller; the press raved about Goldsworthy taking over a number of London West End art galleries in 1994; during 1995 Goldsworthy designed a set of Royal Mail stamps and had a show at the British Museum. Malpas surveys all of Goldsworthy's art, and analyzes his relation with other land artists such as Robert Smithson, Walter de Maria, Richard Long and David Nash, and his place in the contemporary British art scene.

The Art of Andy Goldsworthy discusses all of Goldsworthy's important and recent exhibitions and books, including the *Sheepfolds* project; the TV documentaries; *Wood* (1996); the New York Holocaust memorial (2003); and Goldsworthy's collaboration on a dance performance.

Illustrations: 70 b/w, 1 colour. 330 pages. New, special, 2nd edition.
Publisher: Crescent Moon Publishing. Distributor: Gardners Books.

ISBN 1-86171-059-3 (9781861710598) (Paperback) £25.00 / $44.00

ISBN 1-86171-080-1 (9781861710802) (Hardback) £60.00 / $105.00

CRESCENT MOON PUBLISHING

ARTS, PAINTING, SCULPTURE

The Art of Andy Goldsworthy: Complete Works(Pbk)
The Art of Andy Goldsworthy: Complete Works (Hbk)
Andy Goldsworthy in Close-Up (Pbk)
Andy Goldsworthy in Close-Up (Hbk)
Land Art: A Complete Guide
Richard Long: The Art of Walking
The Art of Richard Long: Complete Works (Pbk)
The Art of Richard Long: Complete Works (Hbk)
Richard Long in Close-Up
Land Art In the UK
Land Art in Close-Up
Installation Art in Close-Up
Minimal Art and Artists In the 1960s and After
Colourfield Painting
Land Art DVD, TV documentary
Andy Goldsworthy DVD, TV documentary
The Erotic Object: Sexuality in Sculpture From Prehistory to the Present Day
Sex in Art: Pornography and Pleasure in Painting and Sculpture
Postwar Art
Sacred Gardens: The Garden in Myth, Religion and Art
Glorification: Religious Abstraction in Renaissance and 20th Century Art
Early Netherlandish Painting
Leonardo da Vinci
Piero della Francesca
Giovanni Bellini
Fra Angelico: Art and Religion in the Renaissance

Mark Rothko: The Art of Transcendence
Frank Stella: American Abstract Artist
Jasper Johns: Painting By Numbers
Brice Marden
Alison Wilding: The Embrace of Sculpture

Vincent van Gogh: Visionary Landscapes
Eric Gill: Nuptials of God
Constantin Brancusi: Sculpting the Essence of Things
Max Beckmann
Egon Schiele: Sex and Death In Purple Stockings

Delizioso Fotografico Fervore: Works In Process 1
Sacro Cuore: Works In Process 2
The Light Eternal: J.M.W. Turner
The Madonna Glorified: Karen Arthurs

LITERATURE

J.R.R. Tolkien: The Books, The Films, The Whole Cultural Phenomenon
Harry Potter
Sexing Hardy: Thomas Hardy and Feminism
Thomas Hardy's *Tess of the d'Urbervilles*
Thomas Hardy's *Jude the Obscure*
Thomas Hardy: The Tragic Novels
Love and Tragedy: Thomas Hardy
The Poetry of Landscape in Hardy
Wessex Revisited: Thomas Hardy and John Cowper Powys
Wolfgang Iser: Essays
Petrarch, Dante and the Troubadours
Maurice Sendak and the Art of Children's Book Illustration
Andrea Dworkin
Cixous, Irigaray, Kristeva: The *Jouissance* of French Feminism
Julia Kristeva: Art, Love, Melancholy, Philosophy, Semiotics and Psychoanalysis
Hélene Cixous I Love You: The *Jouissance* of Writing
Luce Irigaray: Lips, Kissing, and the Politics of Sexual Difference
Peter Redgrove: Here Comes the Flood
Peter Redgrove: Sex-Magic-Poetry-Cornwall
Lawrence Durrell: Between Love and Death, East and West
Love, Culture & Poetry: Lawrence Durrell
Cavafy: Anatomy of a Soul
German Romantic Poetry: Goethe, Novalis, Heine, Hölderlin, Schlegel, Schiller
Feminism and Shakespeare
Shakespeare: Selected Sonnets
Shakespeare: Love, Poetry & Magic
The Passion of D.H. Lawrence
D.H. Lawrence: Symbolic Landscapes
D.H. Lawrence: Infinite Sensual Violence
Rimbaud: Arthur Rimbaud and the Magic of Poetry
The Ecstasies of John Cowper Powys
Sensualism and Mythology: The Wessex Novels of John Cowper Powys
Amorous Life: John Cowper Powys and the Manifestation of Affectivity (H.W. Fawkner)
Postmodern Powys: New Essays on John Cowper Powys (Joe Boulter)
Rethinking Powys: Critical Essays on John Cowper Powys
Paul Bowles & Bernardo Bertolucci
Rainer Maria Rilke
In the Dim Void: Samuel Beckett
Samuel Beckett Goes into the Silence
André Gide: Fiction and Fervour
Jackie Collins and the Blockbuster Novel
Blinded By Her Light: The Love-Poetry of Robert Graves
The Passion of Colours: Travels In Mediterranean Lands
Poetic Forms
The Dolphin-Boy

POETRY

The Best of Peter Redgrove's Poetry
Peter Redgrove: Here Comes The Flood
Peter Redgrove: Sex-Magic-Poetry-Cornwall
Ursula Le Guin: Walking In Cornwall
Dante: Selections From the Vita Nuova
Petrarch, Dante and the Troubadours
William Shakespeare: Selected Sonnets
Blinded By Her Light: The Love-Poetry of Robert Graves
Emily Dickinson: Selected Poems
Emily Brontë: Poems
Thomas Hardy: Selected Poems
Percy Bysshe Shelley: Poems
John Keats: Selected Poems
D.H. Lawrence: Selected Poems
Edmund Spenser: Poems
John Donne: Poems
Henry Vaughan: Poems
Sir Thomas Wyatt: Poems
Robert Herrick: Selected Poems
Rilke: Space, Essence and Angels in the Poetry of Rainer Maria Rilke
Rainer Maria Rilke: Selected Poems
Friedrich Hölderlin: Selected Poems
Arseny Tarkovsky: Selected Poems
Arthur Rimbaud: Selected Poems
Arthur Rimbaud: A Season in Hell
Arthur Rimbaud and the Magic of Poetry
D.J. Enright: By-Blows
Jeremy Reed: Brigitte's Blue Heart
Jeremy Reed: Claudia Schiffer's Red Shoes
Gorgeous Little Orpheus
Radiance: New Poems
Crescent Moon Book of Nature Poetry
Crescent Moon Book of Love Poetry
Crescent Moon Book of Mystical Poetry
Crescent Moon Book of Elizabethan Love Poetry
Crescent Moon Book of Metaphysical Poetry
Crescent Moon Book of Romantic Poetry
Pagan America: New American Poetry

MEDIA, CINEMA, FEMINISM and CULTURAL STUDIES

J.R.R. Tolkien: The Books, The Films, The Whole Cultural Phenomenon
Harry Potter
Cixous, Irigaray, Kristeva: The *Jouissance* of French Feminism
Julia Kristeva: Art, Love, Melancholy, Philosophy, Semiotics and Psychoanalysis
Luce Irigaray: Lips, Kissing, and the Politics of Sexual Difference
Hélène Cixous I Love You: The *Jouissance* of Writing
Andrea Dworkin
'Cosmo Woman': The World of Women's Magazines
Women in Pop Music
Discovering the Goddess (Geoffrey Ashe)
The Poetry of Cinema
The Sacred Cinema of Andrei Tarkovsky (Pbk and Hbk)
Paul Bowles & Bernardo Bertolucci
Media Hell: Radio, TV and the Press
An Open Letter to the BBC
Detonation Britain: Nuclear War in the UK
Feminism and Shakespeare
Wild Zones: Pornography, Art and Feminism
Sex in Art: Pornography and Pleasure in Painting and Sculpture
Sexing Hardy: Thomas Hardy and Feminism

In my view *The Light Eternal* is among the very best of all the material I read on Turner. (Douglas Graham, director of the Turner Museum, Denver, Colorado)

The Light Eternal is a model monograph, an exemplary job. The subject matter of the book is beautifully organised and dead on beam. (Lawrence Durrell)

It is amazing for me to see my work treated with such passion and respect. (Andrea Dworkin)

Sex-Magic-Poetry-Cornwall is a very rich essay... It is like a brightly-lighted box. (Peter Redgrove)

CRESCENT MOON PUBLISHING
P.O. Box 393, Maidstone, Kent, ME14 5XU, United Kingdom.
01622-729593 (UK) 01144-1622-729593 (US) 0044-1622-729593 (other territories)
cresmopub@yahoo.co.uk   www.crescentmoon.org.uk